WHAT MONSTERS YOU MAKE OF THEM

WHAT MONSTERS YOU MAKE OF THEM

poems

CHRISTIAN TERESI

Red Hen Press | *Pasadena, CA*

Book design by Mark E. Cull.

Library of Congress Cataloging-in-Publication Data

Names: Teresi, Christian, author.
Title: What monsters you make of them: poems / Christian Teresi.
Other titles: What monsters you make of them (Compilation)
Description: First edition. | Pasadena, CA: Red Hen Press, 2024.
Identifiers: LCCN 2023054486 (print) | LCCN 2023054487 (ebook) | ISBN
   9781636281704 (trade paperback) | ISBN 9781636281711 (ebook)
Subjects: LCGFT: Poetry.
Classification: LCC PS3620.E738 W47 2024 (print) | LCC PS3620.E738
   (ebook) | DDC 811/.6—dc23/eng/20231130
LC record available at https://lccn.loc.gov/2023054486
LC ebook record available at https://lccn.loc.gov/2023054487

The National Endowment for the Arts, the Los Angeles County Arts Commission, the Ahmanson Foundation, the Dwight Stuart Youth Fund, the Max Factor Family Foundation, the Pasadena Tournament of Roses Foundation, the Pasadena Arts & Culture Commission and the City of Pasadena Cultural Affairs Division, the City of Los Angeles Department of Cultural Affairs, the Audrey & Sydney Irmas Charitable Foundation, the Meta & George Rosenberg Foundation, the Albert and Elaine Borchard Foundation, the Adams Family Foundation, Amazon Literary Partnership, the Sam Francis Foundation, and the Mara W. Breech Foundation partially support Red Hen Press.

First Edition
Published by Red Hen Press
www.redhen.org

To my parents.

Jerry & Joseph Teresi

CONTENT

I

Reading Osip Mandelstam in Zion National Park 13

An Alternate Version of Goya's *The Dog* 16

Climb a Tree, Take a Swim, Kiss a Woman 18

Terms of Surrender 20

Sonny Rollins Explains the Apocrypha to Judas 21

Imperative Pleasures of Coastal Somalia 22

Words in a Dead Girl's Mouth 24

II

The Wreck of the Unknown 29

For the Kingdom to Be Well 30

Mike Tyson Explains Middle Age to John Keats 32

Etymology of Hedberg's Escalator 34

What Monsters You Make of Them

    I. Delight of Gods and Men 36

    II. Zoology 38

    III. Bodies, Again 40

The Quieting Muses 42

The Nine Mayan Gods of the Underworld Explain Delusions to John Roberts . 44

Calculations on the Known World after the Garden of Eden 46

III

Like Shining from Shook Foil 49

IV

Etymology of the Ancient City 69

We Call It Wisdom 72

Reading Nadezhda Mandelstam in Virgin Islands National Park . . . 74

Emina R. Explains the Reflected Past to Christian Teresi 76

Metamorphoses 78

Reading Carlos Drummond de Andrade in Everglades National Park . . 79

Encomium Post Requiem 82

Sibylline 83

To Burn the Autocrat in Effigy 86

Ruth Stone Explains the Book of the Dead to Sylvia Plath 88

Notes 91

Acknowledgments 97

WHAT MONSTERS YOU MAKE OF THEM

I

Crimes da terra, como perdoá-los?
Tomei parte em muitos, outros escondi.
Alguns achei belos, foram publicados.
Crimes suaves, que ajudam a viver.
Ração diária de erro, distribuída em casa.
Os ferozes padeiros do mal.
Os ferozes leiteriros do mal.

How can I forgive the world's crimes?
I took part in many. Others I concealed.
Some I found beautiful, and they were published.
Soothing crimes, which make life more bearable.
A daily ration of error, delivered at our door.
By ruthless milkmen of evil.
By ruthless bread boys of evil.

—Carlos Drummond de Andrade,
    "A Flor e a Náusea," translated by Richard Zenith

READING OSIP MANDELSTAM IN ZION NATIONAL PARK

The river that carved a valley from the sandstone barely changed
Since the first curious landsman walked astonished into the canyon

Eight thousand years later we live with the decisions of bureaucrats
And missionaries who ignored and redacted the indigenous words

Renamed this place after the Jerusalem fortress David conquered
Renamed after the place nearest the divine palace of his Lord

Not at the palace but as close as possible to its celestial dazzle
Not at the palace but as close to the revelations as permitted

———————

Climb from the level morning stairs worn or blasted into riven cliffs
Pilgrims in sparse miniature below will reach this height and forget

The quaint vulgarity of human architecture has no blueprint for this
Condors with ten-foot wingspans wheel through stringent daylight

To them no one looks much bigger than the scurrying chipmunks
That arrived at their misappropriated name from the Ojibwe word

Some Englishman thought sounded similar to *chit* and *mink*
Climb from the level morning stairs worn or blasted into riven cliffs

———————

Lookouts lumber over the rust-beige ombre of slickrock and the words
Of the murdered Russian whose plateaus loom and fingers cling

To any lofty crag large enough for parched and twisted toeholds
Mulling the rituals of apparatchiks who renamed Petersburg to Leningrad

In this loge apart from interrogators whose windowless rooms only open
By forced confession the blessed biting-sweet scent of pinyon admits

That someone thought tourists would never want to visit this place
If they could not pronounce the indigenous words for the river canyon

———————

When exiled Mandelstam knew Saint John at Patmos wrote the Book
Of Revelations in a cave not frighted by its seduction or his banishment

His residence capitulated to the words lowered under lamplight
Here is a dogeared and torn 1975 used copy of out-of-print poems

Bought first by a high school librarian in Texarkana Texas who knew

No meek student at this overlook could be exiled from anywhere

AN ALTERNATE VERSION OF GOYA'S *THE DOG*

We look at what could be your dog drowning.
We came through room after room where there was only the divine
As best guessed. Jesus was never the same

From one canvas to the next. You believe one day our dog will die,
But Goya's dog is a long time in the luxury of undying—
The perpetual mid-paddle, the forever abiding no motion

Tethered to our vexed moment. We tell ourselves we know pretty,
But most we're right where someone said stay. With Goya's dog
All the handsome colors are conjured without bone or fur

Or pain. This is the liminal tour of a limited world you choose
To place your pathos. We look at the painting and see
Your dog barking louder than necessary, or his begging devotion,

Though there is none of those things. We see a lunatic tide
Though there is none. We look, and we look again,
Just as some look at those other paintings and see—and see

An idea of heaven even though they look to me like drowning.
Here the dog is drowning in the dark edges of the day.
Here he is drowning in love. And here, to be fair, he is drowning

In someone's mongrel gaze. Here drowning, come darkness—

Lay down water, dear clever Spaniard—sit and stay

Swimmers floating in the joy of anything, even sorrow.

CLIMB A TREE, TAKE A SWIM, KISS A WOMAN

I am chased by words I love written by a poet
In prison for murder. He will be buried just outside

The concrete and razor-wire walls. A guard tower
Will shade his grave. He writes longingly of the red earth

Of his youth. The landscapes of flowers and rhythms
Of livestock taken to market. He laments he will never

Climb a tree, take a swim, kiss a woman again. He covets
The *harvest,* said in the old way before the word *autumn*

Gained favor. Said by hands that sowed their own satisfaction.
The man's words describe the rippled wood an elder spent

All day carving. Its ceremony is lost to him. The three-year-old
He stabbed to death will never climb a tree, take a swim,

Kiss a woman again. I am halfway gone to the old scripture
Or a mugshot of an artist kept as an icon that makes me

Kneel to not knowing. The boy would be twenty-nine today.
He is never to proffer the names of all-stars in schoolyards

And speak as if dirt is a penance washing grief away. Never
To shout about how blessed he is to divine from what is found

In junk drawers to set fire to boredom. See him navigate
Through lake snow that dresses the ancient city silvery-white.

See his children sled down the hillside thinking their life
Has never been this precarious. In Velázquez's portrait

Of Saint John writing the Book of Revelations from exile
On the island of Patmos, both image and vision appear

Where scripture is lacking—where the page is blank.
For Velázquez, image is meaning when there are no words.

TERMS OF SURRENDER

. . . let us temper our criticism with kindness. None of us comes fully equipped. —Carl Sagan

Let us temper our criticism with
Words bridled by illiterate poets

Never pray over altars of the self
Where no congregants dwell or echo back

Recall sentry who allowed safe passage
Across irrigated fields cleared of stones

May leave half-eaten fruit that wilts then rots.
Kindness. None of us comes fully equipped.

Forgive me for all my half-eaten fruit.
Nor a smug demon slaughtered by belief.

A great refuge was alleged on the moon.
They wintered submerged in warm riverbeds

Roosting to return from the far afield
Still the common falsehoods perch skillfully

Words bridled by illiterate poets.
Never pray over altars of the self.

Where no congregants dwell or echo back.
Recall sentry who allowed safe passage.

Across irrigated fields cleared of stones.
Pests may nibble leaves or cause sallow rot—

May half be plenty for them to leave with
Forgive me for all my half-eaten fruit.

They were not the milestone I believed,
Once, some claimed birds migrated to the moon.

Others said birds slumbered in riverbeds.
Roosting to reappear from the farfetched.

Birds navigate by what seems phantom skills.
Because none of us comes fully equipped.

SONNY ROLLINS EXPLAINS THE APOCRYPHA TO JUDAS

What may have and never did are ordained. I had to damn near quit
Audiences. They demand history as a thing to be tamed. They interpret

Solace in the diminutive—the muted myths made for them. Crowds
Want music that stands between the pregnant woman and the gun—

Even when the music is shot in the leg for its foolishness and bleeds out.
Motherfuckers kill songs and raise others because they're easier to sing.

Your song was made short enough to guarantee you'd swing as little
As possible. Your song choked off by rope so what was will behave.

Give me my horn. Blessings of my left hand and devotions of my right
Are pleading. Some deny they heard, but the breathless remember.

And remember—tell them—I don't care whose life they're trying to prop.
If all they want is to feel like they hear the past, or reckon simple noise

Because it's easier to repeat—the record is always a vague approximation—
Let the way they part with the song be. The end has never been the end.

IMPERATIVE PLEASURES OF COASTAL SOMALIA

Lord of what will happen as if already happened—
Measure cloud cover by all that it hides.

Measure meridians muddled by dead pastures
Where no one survives but by faith, by luck.

Watch desert coordinates as the useless witness.
See a girl. See a stadium with chalk lines for another game.

Play something anyway for the audience waiting.
Count their heads as all the periods in a prayer book

Without any words. Know how well a stone fits in the palm,
And though the shadow of the stone is known,

Know it is impossible for the ill-equipped eye to follow
The stone along this invisible tether to purpose.

Not part of a strong foundation or wall,
Not weak to wear down slowly into sand,

But give the stone some exercise.
Smell salt from the sea the same way the spectators

Easily through redundancy forget the smell of salt.

If when rung let applause pitch out toward the faint parade

Of where water sprays and seeps into the sand

Again and again. See the girl's mouth endlessly unquenchable

With stones. Say, be good and how to be good.

WORDS IN A DEAD GIRL'S MOUTH

I return as Father's prayers that no longer try
To convince him the Lord is kind and merciful.

I cannot return by miracle, as the plastic invention
Working to heal frustration from daily chores.

And not when Father eyes Venus, who always returns,
But distantly in the arc of sleepless hours. I return

As Mother tinkers with muted dangers she forgot
To explain. Someone let me leap from the porch,

And I thought this made me everything except a target
Lead obliges. Singing as an unending amputation

I always return. Even if I could, I doubt there is money
For such things. So, I return the well-known secret

Of the uninvited emissary. Each day, my parents return
To what pays them—just as someone paid someone

To fix the lead with powder, and some showoff boy
Struck it with a hammer. And it arrived as if begging,

As if excited for my blood spreading earnestly

As twilight beneath a futile streetlamp.

II

ma per trattar del ben ch'i' vi trovai,
dirò de l'altre cose ch'i' v'ho scorte.

but to discuss the good I found there,
I must tell you about the other things I saw.

—Dante Alighieri, *Inferno*, Canto I

THE WRECK OF THE UNKNOWN

To the memory of four migrants drowned in the Rio Grande the evening of May 1, 2019.

Walking from home for the unknown distance
   The whole world crosses with little but breath

   Through bedraggled cloudbursts of recalling
Where the landscape nurtures the in-between

   Through orchards fed on the disappeared
      Faith is the geography of elsewhere

   An accord of endurance and daylight.
   And agents daily interpret the land—

Deface shore splitting from tattered shore—
   Footprints wither in the skittering wash—

All maul-swung, all swollen, all deft current—
   The fathomless ride adrift a sodden float

   Appear conjoined to sternly lie ahull.
   Schoolgirl grasps her brother in exodus

The whole world crosses with little but breath.
Through bedraggled cloudbursts of recalling.

Where the landscape nurtures the in-between.
Through orchards fed on the disappeared.

Faith is the geography of elsewhere.
With a choir of endurance and sight—

Walking from home for the unknown distance
Deface shore splitting from tattered shore.

A rippled reflection wades in the wash.
All moving, all formless, all deft current.

The displaced riders of its shrewd float.
Arrive joined to the flecked ends of the hull—

Father holds his infant in exodus.
And agents daily interpret the land.

FOR THE KINGDOM TO BE WELL

Plaques around the zoo claim that during the siege the residents did not eat the animals.

After all the birds, rats, and pets were gone, there was warmth
Over the gnawing sound the body makes when no longer

Fooled by cakes of water, sawdust, and imagination. They looked
Skyward at the useless creatures made of stars. Bright rockets

Screamed, splintered bone, some escaped to somewhere still
Cut too close and closer still. There was where the saw caught,

Goes tough, then continued writhing through the bone. There was
What little drink and humor was left to share. The zookeeper gave,

Butchered the wonderful mammals whose bellies ached more
For unbound grassland, and ached for the minutes between birth

And walking when their mothers licked their slick bodies to get back
Some nourishment they had given. They devoured what they had

Cared for sometimes. Joy was unworkable, so they consumed it
With hours spent neglecting funerals. No longer was there use

For the sunken spectacle of exposed ribs, and they laughed skyward
At the creatures made of stars. Beasts ate other beasts, and flowers

For occasions became dreamlike. The bricks and beams of rubble
Were hymns. Out of the clicking sound of winter were hymns.

MIKE TYSON EXPLAINS MIDDLE AGE TO JOHN KEATS

Sometimes I think I said everything I had to say by twenty-six.
At the reform school, at fifteen, I could take any adult one-on-one.

When it took several of them to take me to solitary, they said
That was what needed to happen for forgiveness. They wanted me

To confess, but I never knew for what. A curse is also sacred, right
John? Stablekeeper's kids know broken then healed, but healed

With limits to how much anything can be set right. You Keats boys
Had minds of feral dreams never bullied into errands for hoodlums.

I've stepped off planes in Istanbul, in Brussels, in Tokyo where
Everyone heard of me. They gave me a parade in Moscow,

But I was still the kid that robbed drug dealers since it was better
When cops had me palms reaching across the hood of their car

To let them take the fifteen hundred in my pocket than take me away.
Your brothers didn't care about poetry, but if you needed to fight

They needed to fight, and that leeway is honest and closefisted.
Your brothers were the song the enemy sings when they warn children

Of the beasts that eat other beasts. You were a monster amazed
At the *moonlight*. I wish I knew what it was like to trust, *These men*

Say things which make one start, without making one feel. Men still
Say dumb things about you, John. They get your dispatches all wrong—

Try so hard to find attention through slick abstraction. What was there
In North London, or Brownsville, Brooklyn, except not to consider

An opponent's size and strength—to know how to get inside
And open like a sonofabitch. Most men must take a few punches

To win, but not you and me, John. We went to the body, to the head
In previously unseen combinations. Still, we move beyond weakness,

Endure lessons of failure. Forgive opponents. Each blow from our hands
Was pity surviving, was survival. How hard men work for imperfection.

ETYMOLOGY OF HEDBERG'S ESCALATOR

I like an escalator, man. Because an escalator can never break. It can only become stairs.
    —Mitch Hedberg

It can never break. It can only become stairs,
Like when I utter words and their vestige becomes

A language borrowed from wooded blooms that wilt
Unnoticed without desire. *It* from Old Blooms,

Meaning whose fragrance wilts, and whose waving
Branches send petals to rappel loss. See

Rappel from French, meaning to recall, or Old French,
Rapeler, a drumroll to summon soldiers. I recall

Telling you about the imperfect collapse of it
Into an old story that plots by failing. Its purpose

Falls away to ground where small animals root
To eat its flesh. They spread it seeds in their scat

That grow to become wooded for small animals.
For it is a museum of becoming that holds

In its collection the steps Gene Kelly scaled *Singing*

In the Rain while he had a fever of 103. That dance

Can never break, it can only shake loose of celluloid

And rise from memory into a measure of birdsong

Ascending from it to escape the wooded void

At the moment of loss. This story is a relic of telling

What is lost and found in the uneven stairs of becoming

It from the Middle French, *escalade*, meaning

To assault a fortified it using ladders to scale

The walls. Townsfolk wilted inside the gates as soldiers

Shed parts of their flesh no longer needed by this story.

This story of loss, from the Old Norse, *los*, meaning

To breakup an army. Except armies can only be armies

Or folks who in bloom become a kindness, a comedy.

WHAT MONSTERS YOU MAKE OF THEM

I. DELIGHT OF GODS AND MEN

She reminds him of goblins, of flowers
That smell of laughter as they burn.
Heaven is shaped in different ways.

He recites incantations of fancy
Is the same as fear. He says to her
It is okay to be steadied by fiction.

He lets happiness ride through him
As a clamped teething thing.
Held to the bright hook of darkness,

Persephone pilfers an appetite
For luck and warmth. She would lose everything
If only to salvage the south-leaning light.

Hades alternates instantly
Between fussing and falling asleep.
He prattles, cradles her, and jokes—

All gods lack aptitude, but at least he is not cruel

Enough to name his garden Pleasure

And kick everyone out when they wanted any.

II. ZOOLOGY

She read in the paper where faraway they cut the hands
From thieves. She thinks if his hands were removed
They'd grow back with a more tangled reach.

She read in the paper where the judge called him
An animal—and as if to disprove the claim he replied,
I am not an animal. She suspects nothing natural holds

On to vulnerability with nostalgia, and tries to forget how
Her hands feel tethered to her uncle who is four legs, two legs,
Baying and talking. Even when caged he invests in the passion

Of natures. He strolls and hums an old limping tune
For his niece and the three other girls. He warms himself
Inside a coat, walks the yard, and sees them. The verdict

Was not enough to steal them away. He spends his minutes
Missing their cool sweetness. Alone in his cell he thinks
He did not do enough to baffle Hades or oblige him.

She thinks of her uncle, and he thinks of her as clothing
For his naked heart. The girls cure him even as their likeness
Sours in his mind. He hopes they are pleased.

He calls, *darlings*, to love in dresses, spinning, dancing
On Saturday night, *treat me well*, in moments of make-believe.
Truss yourself to the stories teachers tell.

III. BODIES, AGAIN

I am reminded of what I already know. Every posture
Married to the needs of animals. The counselor is earnest
About her tired shuffle, says, *Decay is a difficult thing to whip.*

On the last day K is present in class, I teach Greek myths
Then walk an almost empty hallway and hear this argument—
But, I love you. Marcus replies, *You ho. You'd suck anyone's cock*

I told you to. Marcus looks at me, grabs the space between us,
Lectures, *she would you know,* affirming not the farce of his mother
Calling him prince, or K's abuse—but my helplessness having known

What had been going on for weeks. Marcus picks K up and they drive—
Friends' houses, fast food, go and see a movie. She does everything
She thinks is love—unzips, unbuttons, plays secretly in not-so-secret places.

K, who after her mother kicked her out, confides, *and don't tell anyone,*
She's pregnant. Two months later the boy is different, but again,
I'm pregnant. K rouses difficulties less resigned to desperate—conjures

The reproductive cycle of a fruit bat—imagines something belongs to her

That cannot be claimed by another. Even by example the intangible,

As in class I ask her to imagine how Demeter languishes and weeps

Unchecked as she calls into the pit for her daughter. K believes fantasies

Make a home, or opportunity, or spring—believes by the failure

That makes a pomegranate seed some terrible consummation.

THE QUIETING MUSES

Some words breathless, bait then snare. Some
Scry in the mysteries of their snarled limbs.

Some words are conjured only to be wary
Of silence. *Silence is more honest than speaking,*

Said Miles Davis, his rasp telling Coltrane
About the solos—*Why do you play so long?*

Coltrane said he could never find a good place
To stop. *Well, you could just take the horn*

Out of your mouth. There is no gamble
Except, breathless, the blue-pitched ocean carries

All the expanse of nothing to say. When called
Distantly, spectrally, tides swell and disappear

Into nowhere pronounceable. From their source
They skiff the reflection of attended moons

Over the drift of scales and flash. Signals
Derived from the loam of ageless dynamos

We do not understand. All our monuments

Point achingly toward the sky where stands

The memory of the maw—that tears evolved

As a means of communication before language.

THE NINE MAYAN GODS OF THE UNDERWORLD EXPLAIN DELUSIONS TO JOHN ROBERTS

What unique perspective does a minority student bring to a physics class?

    —Chief Justice John Roberts, US Supreme Court, *Fisher v. Texas*, December 9, 2015

We know the place you were once innocent—without

The protection of lies. Without power that each time revealed

Incrementally celebrated the not-really and never-were.

What passed coolly over river rock—fused between

Unnamed prairie and unknown delta—still stretches

Unbroken without a need for proclamation. You called

For the dead dog because toddlers do not understand death.

When Cortés arrived off the coast of Mexico, he ordered

A native brought to his ship, as he believed was the right

Of the conquistador. Cortés asked his Mayan captive.

Ma c'uhah than, the man replied, and the Spanish first heard

Yucatán, the place of their discovery, where *Ma c'uhah than*

Means, "I do not understand you." We have heard

The song of warriors who taunt and boast with trinkets

They believe must be taken from the dispossessed
And busted inside out by boredom and bootheels if only

To scare confessions from their captives' throats. Soldiers
Protected by pretend. We would not speak than speak

Of scatterings where tyrants forget they wear the old veils.
Be ancient, a forgotten language satisfied with being lost.

CALCULATIONS ON THE KNOWN WORLD AFTER THE GARDEN OF EDEN

The Lord will fight for you; you have only to be still. —Exodus 14:14

You can only tell your heart so long be still. The rural minister said,
The load we share is rooted in the Tree of Knowledge. He said,

Beware your simple acts. The minister and his family die instantly.
What is not yours to take, he asked. A fig taken down from the Tree

Brought bodily pleasure. He said, love can be found in the body.
Love can be lost. Pain can be found in the body. Be still. Be still.

Driving home after services the minister and his family die.
What the Tree tells us is once you know you cannot unknow.

Don't fault the barn owl for the field mice, he said. We must wait
To be free of the body, and we sin. After two centuries, a tree upends

To crush a car. We must say to our heart be still as if as uncertain
About the next breath as some small animal trembling in the underbrush.

III

οὐκ ἔστι λαθεῖν, ὅτε μὴ χρήζων
θεὸς ἐκκλέπτει.

There is no secrecy, except the secrecy of revelations.

—Euripides, *Ion*

Say the bones are saved with the help of thousands of hands. From deep furrows of callused dirt, and the folded scuffle of dactyl-roots—the rummage that grips what others forsake. What goes away never stays away and returns just as the day turns a rabbit out from the thicket. From beneath the silt and soil—the amniotic muck—the souls of things arrive grimy and breathing.

Out of the darkness in the field—that distant hollow flanked by dusk—where there should only have been corn, a birch caught the breeze and quickened with the gusts.

Where the clearing hand had stopped—where the farmer said enough of what I need —the remaining stand held on from where they'd seen their group pared back.

Start with a path worn by walking, then horses, then cut and fit for a road, then some structures (clapboard mostly). Where squatters were, they stayed, they built.

When the road was still rut and dirt and no neighbor was near, a farmer built a house, a barn, cleared more land, planted some crops. A boy paused to jump and pull at birch branches. Say the seeds move with the help of thousands of hands.

When the farmer's family was gone the townspeople speculated. *They offended a higher spirit. They got what they deserved. It's just a damn shame.*

The house was untouched. Everything in its place. The lever on the pump rested half-cocked. Wood waited to be stacked and seasoned. A half set of mail-order china in the cabinet. The girls' clothes folded in dressers made by hand.

A boy paused but came looking to play with Emily. From the porch he called, once, twice. He pulled the latch holding the storeroom door and found the dog. He took a step into the living room. The floor was stained red to brown in a long uneven swath.

Relatives came and took what they could. The girls' clothes for cousins. The china for an aunt. The wood stove and a pair of Holsteins auctioned. A boy kept the dog, *To ease what he'd seen.*

Years of this build and tear down. Say never anything resembling a church, though not much is needed to sing a hymn or kneel and pray.

Sitting on the porch steps all afternoon is a prayer; and plowing the fields—sweat is some kind of providence. When you are thirsty dishwater is as good as holywater—is a certain belief.

> A turning, a winding on a particularly dangerous stretch of Berkshire backroad. She smiles, points to some birch trees, *Do you think they feel pain?* Down through the drift they drive in the mind-set of the maple-man as bloodletter. The trees stand in pale bottom nakedness, their yellow pants swept around their ankles.

Early September. Some boys from town dared each other to go in. The rooms emptied. The pump removed from the well. The boys threw stones through windows. Weeds were tall where firewood had been strewn in the yard. The cats turned feral. Corn massed in the field then rotted where it rose. Mice multiplied.

Margaret and Emily played in the kitchen while their father planted lilac bushes. One for each side of the porch steps. One for each of them. They could hear the shovel piling dirt in soft falls. Emily went through the picture book and stopped to point at the duck-billed platypus and elephant as proof. The priest may never talk about it, but God is an awfully funny guy.

Say the bones are forgotten; the birch now whiter than fog over the field that was always a field even when what grew was from no discernable hand.

On the edge of the field was a home of birch. And hence? A team of oxen? A John Deere engine? An ax *thwack*?

Just a damn shame, for something to be put away, that it's not yours unless you've broken it, until it's lost its novelty, its newness.

The warranty seems to have been thrown out with the box, but that's simply the cost of business with handshakes.

Margaret said anyone would be funny if they had an infinite sense of humor, and infinite laughter, and an infinite audience. If she was infinite, Margaret hesitated, maybe Thomas Boyle would like her. Emily made a face at the mention of the Boyle boy but was curious.

Not the platypus, not the boy, nothing seemed as funny to Emily as the drawing of icebergs. What nonsense, a piece of ice the size of a house and built in the middle of nowhere for no reason.

The sisters agreed, it was hard to distinguish between when God is laughing with you and when God is laughing at you. Emily wanted to ask her father, but Margaret said she shouldn't. *God may be funny, but when do you ever hear him laugh? Daddy wouldn't know anyway.*

> Where the road left the one-bar, one-store, one-school towns, there was
> smooth asphalt for people who had to get through without stopping.
> *Do you wonder if they care to know anything different?* Swiftly they go
> by a dirty child playing on the side of the road.

That first winter snow edged through broken windows and drifted down the entranceway from room to room. Room to room, white as bone that sits in a corner all day then rises suddenly and shifts as if an unmerciful tantrum. From one storm a few birch trees fell from the weight and in the spring remained uncleared in the field.

The bones that hold skin in place are no lovelier than sinews that root and grasp mud and stones—anything really—placed here or there for no particular reason.

For what is a brick but a big toe? What is a floor but walking?

Say the paradigm of heaven is nonsense. God gets around; *he even sleeps with the ugly ones.*

What is a building but a stand-and-stare with the eyes of windows? What are the joist and collar beams but bones?

Unheard, secure with nonsense, a chanting in tongues. A bone used to beat a drum.

What is the nebula but the knowledge and soul of an unbelievable fairytale?

There are ways of believing that go beyond the senses. Tonight, someone is dancing.

This is not moldering. This is gathered and saved once for the turning, once for re-turning. A break in the bend of a tree line—a path made to walk.

Margaret sat on the porch steps knitting all afternoon. Emily played with the dog and half-listened to her mother read to her father from a week-old paper. Say what she heard was, *The body of the vortex was miles to the southwest, but the winds were enough to lift the eaves of the roof.*

Emily stopped playing. *The winds were enough to lift the eaves of the roof and spread an odd shadow across the kitchen floor.* The dog pushes his nose at her hand, but she heard, *Outside three decades of cottonwoods wretched then snapped as if torn by a giant unseen fist.*

Her mother said—the dog half-listened—and what she heard—*One child seized a locket from her bedroom; one child gazed at the barnyard full of panic-stricken animals; one child yelled for the dog.*

Her mother said and Emily heard—*From across the kitchen floor one stared in denial at her mother; one took her face into her hands silently and cried.*

Newspaper got the woodstove going. The girls help their mother with dinner.

They whispered in their room long after bedtime. Emily's mind shuddered when her sister said, *God may not even be the name of God.*

After Margaret fell asleep the moon hunched sideways through the tops of trees and Emily thought no name was better than another—if she got sick of saying God she would say Hank, or Herb, or Hannah.

The harvest woods whip by on either side of the road. The fractured light through the branches frames something for her eyes. *You see those lilac bushes? There must have been a house there. Lilac doesn't grow wild like that.*

Between the wind and snow the birch trees had to ease what they could and heaped upon one another. They pointed oddly away from where they stood—limbs torn and twisted. The shadow of where they stood was still a shadow for an other. Not birch, but shadow. Not birch but let them think they're sleeping in the ether. What they were was limp with faces to the ground—hiding something on the underside—bodies piled without much care.

Not a lullaby. Say a hard-coming fairytale.

God loves (and loves and loves) even the ugly things. Hank puts on his best shirt. Hannah wears perfume. Tonight, they will make a little music. Tonight, the floor-boards will clap to their dancing.

Herb would rather make a mess than do nothing. He digs a hole, stops, digs another, and another. He goes to the landing, half-listens, shakes himself dry, warms under the eave, becomes bored—returns to the refuse, puddles, and muck.

Nothing is lonelier than someone who loves all the time. Hannah is never weary of the world or tired of teaching.

There is fire in the mind, in the unbroken breath. *Have patience, you'll feel it.*

. . . loves a mess and loves disorder. Like you, Hank also loves the rain on the roof and church spires in the distance. Why put limits on love? Sometimes all it takes is the thump of boots on a boarded floor.

Sometimes, the mud split ripe and cleaved into the sole.

A honeybee's handiwork elegantly chants in tongues.

Man was formed from the dust of the Earth is what Emily heard the priest say, and she pushed her hands into the soil to see.

If Hannah was going to send her only son to Earth again, could he come as a honeybee? Because why not? *Mind your own bee's wax.*

At the edge of the cornfield Margaret pulled flowers. Always some soul grimy and breathing. Bloodroot for spring. She smelled their perfume. Emily pictured blood held the flowers in place.

When she heard Emily, she went to see, *What are you laughing at?* Emily smiled, turned her hand over, and let loose her hold so dirt could sift loose and return.

No one believes as anyone else believes. And since the house is abandoned—say save the lilac for some child.

Stop me if you've heard this one.

The girls' aunt came to visit when she was almost seven months pregnant. Emily sat silent most of the afternoon cyclically reaching out to touch her stomach. *Be patient, you'll feel it.*

So, one birch says to another birch . . .

The farmer took on a hand from Douglas who one night killed the family and buried them under the floorboards. Nobody knew why except that he loved and loved one daughter.

He stood over Emily as she slept. He watched her jostle slightly before he broke open her neck with a blade her mother used for digging.

White you are.

Say in the wilderness—hear voices or be deafened to the dead.

Early June. Emily walked with the dog on large stones across the low stream. From her mother, the girl knew the rocks had been there a long time.

On one side of the bank were birch trees. Fits of sunlight and high grass filled the space between. Among the grass was a whole congregation of flowers. Emily called them grassflowers.

Grassflowers grew in patches. Where they ended was pasture fence. Hank liked to *Keep things in. Keep things out.* She sat a long time. Distantly, flanked by dusk, the farmhand watched.

Herb liked not to say much or say nothing.

Emily sat with her feet in the water. She would slide them in, watched her ankles go orderless and break at odd angles below the surface. She would pull them back so the light would mend them. The dog sat panting.

The sky was turning a translucent purple. Hannah spilled wine on a light blue tablecloth. Hank took off his work clothes and on his back was the sky bruised but healing. Emily was not supposed to be this far from the house. Herb sniffed at the skin of a plum and knew it was all light underneath.

Emily tried to fathom the gift as her mother termed it. Bleeding where it's not natural. *Every month?* Her mother worried and wrote to her sister.

Herb can love and be loved . . .

> They rise up and down through the mountains with birds rising and drifting. She realizes she may one day forget all she had said—for there are certain mannerisms and moments, certain turns wound and stretched around, certain stretches of road that carry bones, and every twist is a stitch, every bump rides and holds.

Sulking home, every time Emily looked the sky turned different. Before the wash of pitch—Hank's hand mired in engine oil—there was a moment of sepia. Hannah forgets to leave the bedroom door open just a crack.

The farmhand remained where it was easy to watch and not be watched.

Emily turned toward the bend where the path emptied into the field. Once house-lights returned to her it would be too late for the farmhand.

In one motion she heard the dog take off through the woods yelping and was spun down hard into the crook of an exposed root.

The farmhand said, *shush* and *shush* and *it's okay*, and holds his hand over her mouth.

His breath returning to her face. Emily tried to say, *Herb*, oh *Herb*.

The farmhand believed. Emily took off running . . . *where it's not natural*. Hands live with true or false depending on how well they hold.

Say Emily, say, but she could not.

The farmhand believed he was dead but was not. Still breathing hard, he wondered why he heard Emily call the dog.

On the roadside some skid marks and a pile of glass that used to be a windshield. At every stop sign in a hilltown she leans over and half begs until she is happy. *Tell me you love me.*

This was different from the other fluids that made her—mottled underwear, noses treading on shirt cuffs; what dabbed her clothes with indelible stains.

Where blood was found unexpectedly was an augury. Nothing like what came from untied shoelaces or a cracked lip. This was the hayloft when the bottom rung seemed unreachable and corners propelled themselves beyond dimensions she had known.

Emily wanted her mother but could not say.

That night, taking the silences into her hands and bringing them back to her chest, she quietly slipped into bed with Margaret. She did what her mother said to do when hurt, *One, Two, Three*, and swear, *but do it quietly so God doesn't hear you.*

Lies live with true or false depending on how well they're told.

Hannah thinks Herb only half-listens. *Anything you call lazy to their face and get away with it only half-listens.*

The farmhand pulled up the floor and sectioned the parents with an ax, then Margaret. Emily was last. He stroked her hair where it was not matted. He watched her sleeping. This was just another kind of sleeping. These are bones to hold the earth in place.

The floorboards are put back in place.

Herb loves you more from your hand on his head. Every tree, what's more, every leaf, every needle, every *goddamn piece of trash* holds. And love holds.

When light through the window woke him, the farmhand stood from the floor, left open the door to the house, and walked down the road. He looked until the horizon protruded on the edge of a cloud like an arm tattooed with light. The monstrous wealth of sky was purple and pink and blue, and the blue of his mother's apron, and blue, the eye of a calf motionless in the far field after an ice storm—the vein that runs just below the surface—and blue.

Say the ground is woven with bits of root and bone. The ground is woven with the diaphanous swelling of where a birch once was. And loves.

You and you and you. There were birch trees here and here and here. Some branches are torn by a boy pulling.

Hannah sat on Emily's bed and sang quietly. Not a lullaby. Later her husband asked what took so long. *She had a nightmare.*

A birch is felled once. And when you take the ax to a cornfield? The birch you'd swing through, but it is there, even after the ax, even after the hollering rot of a stump has been ripped up by chains.

And the stump? A quarter column from ruins? A seat for a fairy table? Some sculpture for a dilettante?

Birch trees die as birch trees. Stumps as stumps.

People die in houses. They die in railroad yards, barrooms, in hospitals, at an intersection in their best pajamas, and in churches. They die and are never found. They die and are found only after a hotel guest starts to smell something foul.

The sheriff never found the farmhand from Douglas.

All that we know is not all that is laudable.

Make ugly things sound pretty and they will pass. *The twilight hung in the lilac bushes.*

The doctor told the sheriff he would not have found it if she wasn't mutilated. *The girl's only a couple of weeks along.*

Sometimes the heart beats wildly (and loves) for nothing, for nonsense. In the name of the Hank, the Herb, and the Holy Hannah.

The kingdom of Heaven resembles a cottonwood seed, is what her father told her. Emily pictured trees made of cotton.

IV

People pay for what they do, and still more for what they have allowed themselves to become. And they pay for it very simply by the lives they lead.

—James Baldwin, *No Name in the Street*

ETYMOLOGY OF THE ANCIENT CITY

We labor to forget
The trees planted after strip-mining.

We forgot we named them, *Tree
Of Heaven*, to help hide our excess.

We think it mercy to forge one narrative
By removing another. We plant heaven,

Feel blameless but it is cruel. The trees
Also named ghetto palms in the field guide

For troubled things. *Ghetto* thought to be
From the Venetian *Ghet*, meaning waste or slag.

The place where they plant the unwanted.
Island where the Venetians forced them.

Island whose alluvium is washed by the discarded
They named ghetto, maybe from the Gothic

Gatwo, meaning street. The place they lived
By waste and whatever tangles grew

In the false distance. Close enough for work songs
Whose melody lingered when it arrived

As murmurs no longer fluent in their origin.
Living no further from their previous meaning

Than across a canal. In the small hours, impassable
Tides separate one into another. No longer

Concerned with what was said before. *Ghetto*
Cultivated possibly from the Hebrew *Get*,

Meaning a document allowing wives other men
By forced separation. A divorce of the altogether,

Arrived at from the Sumerian, or Aramaic, or words
Lost by degrees imaginably as close to the language

Of heaven as ever permitted. Almost nothing is known
About the people who spoke the original language

Because of their defeat in battle. In the voices
Of their ancient city, which is a variant of any city,

Night arrives from dusk when no one can tell

Between a wolf and a dog in the distance.

WE CALL IT WISDOM

Pain comes from darkness / And we call it wisdom. It is pain.
            —Randall Jarrell

There was delight by the makers—those who collect hand salutes,
Those who value medals and the pleasure of inventing projectiles.

They think it is whimsical to know how the heart is also something
To aim at. They coo to a traditional clamor—sometimes to soothe,

Sometimes to lie. They affirm—without the growl and spit
Of breakneck seas there would not be life rafts, or beacons

To peel away darkness. Without death, we would not have rodeo clowns
To entertain us, or fire escapes to rest houseplants in summer,

But some of the ninth graders laughed sheepishly with excitement
While watching floor slough upon floor on the outdated television.

For some this was more classwork—Newtonian documentary or whatnot—
They could happily ignore. I wanted to explain, but they had already read

Where after each name in the textbook the beginning and the end
Was parenthetical. I tried to tell them, but the floors were discernable

In the way silhouettes are colored by crepuscular shades. The debris
Could not be unpacked by June, despite propaganda that made us something

We wanted to believe we were but were not. About history we forget,
There is the small and airless trivia someone says—ten hours of combat

In a blizzard. Twenty-eight thousand slaughtered at the battle, they say.
Someone believed it was Palm Sunday. Another believed guessing

The name of the battle, and for others this guess became the name
Of the battle. Archaeologists were excited when they found mass graves.

READING NADEZHDA MANDELSTAM IN VIRGIN ISLANDS NATIONAL PARK

Every trinket and provision and provocation arrives
By ships riding over sunken ships few remember.
The sea turtles only surface for air when it is safe.
Time is boats rocking their length against waves.

A wild donkey appreciates petting between old ears
That evolved to be long and upright to better hear
What is imminent. Garish yachts in the turquoise bay
Are also anchored to the animal kingdom but badly.

Hummingbirds glide then hover at the century flower
That blooms only once before it dies. And the desire
Of unseen tree frogs clatters across the bay indifferent
To bow lights lurching closer through the night.

Open air shops sell canvases stained by kitschy pastels.
Icons of donkeys stare from above the bar at lush hotels.
Their likenesses outnumber the herd whose ancestors
Were liberated when slavery ended. Here small vespers

Forever happen amid vistas held by trembling palms.
Remember pigmy goats steeply skitter when alarmed.
Ancestors of the few native residents carved deities
Into basalt below the waterfall to watch in silent fealty.

No one remembers their motive, but there are doubts
It was to beckon sunburned tourists with illusory debates
About the land's lucre. Ruinous sugarcane plantations
Crumble in their unprofitable finale. Among vacations

Too busy counting many kinds of coconut cocktails,
Nadezhda moves haltingly through memory's octaves.
From town to small town, writing without the danger
Of putting any words to paper. She vanishes hours

Before the secret police arrive in abandoned rooms
To arrest her. Remember pigmy goats are memories
Of their ancestors left by pirates as food for when
They erratically return. Eventually they did not return.

EMINA R. EXPLAINS THE REFLECTED PAST TO CHRISTIAN TERESI

There are soldiers sometimes. They are congregants of order
By alarm, wisdom by suspicion. Their warmth probes to find

Where the joint breaks. For my father is one half pleading,
The other stricken with the sight of the empty window angled

From his knees. The soldiers preach collisions to my father
Who is not a solider. He owned a grocery. He wouldn't let them

In front of me. I see a harvest bleeding to winter. Noon to dusk.
When you ask about Bosnia, what I know is we were playing.

Maybe a game the soldiers still play. In the ancient city,
Games honored the virtuous. A golden ring and yards of silk

Given to the victor to bless his home the way sunlight interrogates
Lake water all summer always accusing what September confesses

As steam that veils the distant shore. We are too concerned
With possession, and not enough with what is on the other side

Of the world we hope to make. The ancient city ages by mishap.
There is the before, then after what remains is a foundling—

Both a part of what was and a whole of something new entirely.
From the sky to the lake below, the exodus of steam is reflected

Wraithlike on the water's surface. In the ancient city, I am
The reason—the loser honored with a mirror to look at myself.

METAMORPHOSES

The Naga were headhunters who wrote butterfly
On the parched reliefs of temples and in manuscripts born
By monastics that knew anything meaningful is without speaking.

They wrote butterfly to tell how to find their ancestors.
When they stopped cutting the heads off missionaries, they started
To care about clothes. Some think the Naga are not Naga

If they cannot hunt heads. Some Naga still believe
In were-tigers who travel to the spirit world to speak
With the dead, which is to say they speak with butterflies.

The Naga wrote butterfly, and I still know what they mean.
After enough time, no one remembers who anyone was.
Butterflies are reincarnated dead warriors to some

Or foretell imminent evil to others. The Naga know butterflies
Conjoined to the air as silence is the most meaningful prayer.
No one remembers these ancient ways, but they show something

Of what they were in those words. In the beginning,
There was the way wings sigh and ease down without kneeling.
There was nectar and the migration from one belief to another.

READING CARLOS DRUMMOND DE ANDRADE IN EVERGLADES NATIONAL PARK

Up to 87% of the global wetland resource has been lost since 1700. We lose wetlands three times faster than natural forests. —The Ramsar Convention

On the edge of the park tourists pay to hold the hatchlings
Of the caged ten-foot attraction whose half-burrow leaves little

Room to turn around in the mudpack the way she did waiting
For workers on break to amuse themselves with a bit of peril

Tossing scraps into the canal to gawk at her ravenous contortions
Alligators do not know the difference between food they catch

In the wild where they may wait submerged for forty-five minutes
And food fed to them by workers behind a meat packing plant

———————

So the wildlife commission labels handfed alligators a nuisance
But alligators must be alligators before they can be something else

Before they are the thrill that costs twenty-five dollars per tourist
Or wait at the edge of orchards growing South Asian mangos where

Wetlands were drained and cypress windbreaks culled to plot soil
This is plentiful not for the parade of white pelicans gliding

Not for the mangrove where a night heron in discreet silence looks
Reborn from the afterlife while overhead swifts share the sound

Of six-foot-tall sawgrass rustling in imperceptibly moving water
And the commission orders nuisance alligators must be caged

Or killed simply because they never know the difference between
Wading birds and a toddler who has wobbled too close to the edge

———————————

I am preparing a song to wake the men and lullaby the children
Andrade says in a poem put on the fifty cruzados novo banknote

A small bill to stave off inflation and remind us of a *Canção Amiga*
Friendly Song to bless the money required to pay Brazilian debts

Andrade says but the song never arrives and for preparation we pay
With words used to describe the tide that now has legal definitions

With money made from cotton that grew wild in prehistoric times
Was finished into nets and traded with coastal villages for fish

Money from the Roman title of the Goddess Juno the Protector
Of the State and a word that has the same ancestor as *monitor*

Which is meant to caution you into remembering the expense
To lawfully permit parcels of eternity and forever and everglade

ENCOMIUM POST REQUIEM

Like the last celebrant of an almost forgotten goddess
Held together by worship, the woman I love loves

Her dead grandmother. She annuls impermanence
With a festival of loneliness. Of normalcy,

The woman I love loves the trouble to get back
To what is impossible. She smiles, and whatever was

Goes from the totem of what is still. Love
Like the language an immigrant child is told to forget

But senility brings back before death. Resurrected
In the sugar for an imaginary tea. In the meridian,

Like a half-lit moon, where she is the shadow
In ecstasy chasing the altar of bright migration.

When her empty table is anointed with tangerines.
For some are summoned in sweet offerings.

SIBYLLINE

Outside, in the starry dusk, the wind blew and in its way was the only one to
commemorate the dead.

　　—Giuseppe Tomasi di Lampedusa, *The Leopard*

The dark cosmos calibrates arrival to today
From a spatial dawn so hot it was devoid

Of measurement—except mass brutally unfolding
Across forgotten bodies too stunning for anything

But equations to value. All that arrives is wreckage
From the unobservable distant past that lingers

In misperceptions of hereafter. Even elephants will take
Migratory detours to visit the bones of their dead.

And I arrive to the clockwork of today to find Sibyl
Dead. The ancient priestesses who initiated her name

Were said to divine the future when delirious with song
Or frenzied after inhaling volcanic fumes. They knew

Nothing about how the mass expanded through vague
And diffuse assemblages of primordial flotsam. They were

Surrounded by zealots who believed seers navigated time
And occupied elements of its narrative before they occurred.

Sibyl's incomplete maps of the sky foresaw death
Would arrive a trace of the endless engine that translates

Loneliness into energy into work. Today she died a part
Of the absolute that moves the bending universe in barely

Conceivable purposes that require words for the inexhaustible

as divination. A pursuit of a future

Where all energy everywhere is in equilibrium.   Then   there
Will be no stars, no highly organized matter that depend

On temperature differences to drive their structure.   No
Clouds on Jupiter.   No bubbles lilting   upward   upward

towards their own annihilation   in the infinite
of your Champagne glass.   no rainfall
from thunderstorms   careening down hills to amass

into a flood that moves houses off their foundations.
Sibyl's flesh and heat dissipate

to prove equations of cosmology   yesterday
the hours mattered and the sun passed in normal eruptions

onto fruited vines   today   lonesome mysteries
roost in the flush exposure of burnt hills   and here

Sibyl is gone from where

     entropy   pulls   time   forward   forward
          from our perception
          and   backward   in the mirror

universe that parallels our own

where each side of time lives in the other's deepest past
on the opposite side   of the beginning   Sibyl

lifted from the errors of our reflection   released into the conduit

today   where she is   just   becoming

TO BURN THE AUTOCRAT IN EFFIGY

The garden where his soldiers hanged an old woman
Again smells of petrichor and tomato vines.

His daybook was written by thin-necked deputies.
It will be used as evidence against him.

His name is no longer a punchline spoken secretly.
The branch that held the noose now holds a swing.

No teacher has been burned alive for believing
The earth revolves around the sun for a very long time.

The bomb-shattered windows that littered the schoolyard
Have been replaced. Children again play pretend

Soldiers on the rebuilt playground. They know a young woman
Was found in the house behind the school. They know her name

Was Anna. She was found shot in the head in the potato cellar.
The school is the same one she once attended. Her photo

In the potato cellar wearing nothing but a frayed fur coat
Is used as evidence against him. It wins a prestigious prize

For photography. The school's bomb shelter is now storage

For textbooks. There was a time when books were scarce

And few could read. Children pass the bomb shelter entrance

And do not know what its sign means. The word human

Comes from the Latin, *Humus*, meaning *black earth*.

An old hunting dog dreams it can still catch grouse mid-air.

Generations of crows have lived without tasting human flesh.

Beneath the sickle-shaped moon the earth still revolves

Around the sun. Builders approach the ruins counting

Salvable bricks. The ballerinas never stopped rehearsing.

RUTH STONE EXPLAINS THE BOOK OF THE DEAD TO SYLVIA PLATH

I did what I could to hush the knot and rope, the truth of gravity.
There are not enough idiomatic expressions to converse flawlessly

With the dead. You must let some meaning slide. I could not
Waste energy extinguishing the flicker between the possible

Storms divided by the posture of chemicals in the brain
And prizes awarded to the dead after they have continued

To the next life. If time is spent wondering how care surrenders
Without so much as a mirror to host a vision of the future

This is how time is consumed. Whatever else there is to mark
Passing goes rudderless, becomes a costume without a feted day—

A place where each breath washes the next as waves giving way.
I leave the bed to get the girls into nightgowns, if only so they hear

My forged laughter. Not the sound of the knot slipping to cinched.
Not objects where the dead once saw their reflection, or how

Ink cannot ever say the same as what the mouth sounds.
My students are in rows, alive—day-picked apples cut by teeth—

Sweet and long-time coming. My hair the color of the sun

Fixed over storms of smoke. I am one you see smiling.

NOTES

Reading Osip Mandelstam in Zion National Park. Osip Mandelstam (1891–1938) was first exiled from Leningrad by Stalin in 1934 and then in 1938 sentenced to five years in the gulags where he died. Joseph Brodsky (1940–1996) wrote that Mandelstam was killed because of his "linguistic, and, by implication, his psychological superiority, rather than because of his politics." Those linguistic skills are likely why instructions were first given to "isolate and preserve" him in exile instead of execute him. Zion National Park was first named Mukuntuweap National Monument in 1909 to honor the indigenous Southern Paiute who had long been the inhabitants of the region. Mukutuweap means "straight canyon" in Paiute. The Southern Paiute name for the canyon was "Loogoon" meaning "arrow quiver." The park's name was changed to Zion in 1919 over concerns an indigenous name would deter tourists. Zion was the name used by Mormon settlers. To Josh Baugher (1980–).

An Alternate Version of Goya's *The Dog*. *The Dog* is one of Francisco Goya's (1746–1828) fourteen *Pinturas Negras* (Black Paintings) that he painted directly on the wallpaper of his house outside Madrid between 1819, when he was seventy-two, and 1823. The murals were untitled, and he likely never intended them to be shown publicly. They are now displayed at the Museo del Prado in Madrid. They are some of the most shocking and celebrated works of Goya's career.

Climb a Tree, Take a Swim, Kiss a Woman. In memory of Adrian Brasch (1992–1995). According to the CDC, one in seven children experience abuse or neglect each year in the United States; more than four children die from abuse or neglect in the United States every day. The reference to Velázquez is taken from *Images of the Immaculate Conception and the Rhetoric of Purity in Golden Age Spain* by art historian Rebecca Quinn Teresi (1988–), who wrote, "both image and vision appear precisely where scripture is lacking—where the page is, in fact, blank."

Terms of Surrender. A quadruplex, based on the duplex form invented by Jericho Brown. Within the oral traditions of the ancient world most poets were illiterate. Some antiquity and pre-industrial naturalists believed birds migrated to the moon or slept all winter in riverbeds. While not fully understood, it is believed migratory birds navigate by some combination of being able to sense (or possibly see) the earth's magnetic field, or by using the sun, stars, or natural landmarks as directional cues.

Sonny Rollins Explains the Apocrypha to Judas. Tenor saxophonist Sonny Rollins (1930–) became disillusioned with life as a professional musician and took the first of several sabbaticals from publicly performing from 1959 to 1961; during this period, he could be found practicing almost daily on the Williamsburg Bridge. The Gospel of Judas Iscariot was written by early Christians before 180 AD and portrays its namesake as Jesus' closest confidant who only followed his teacher's orders by betraying him. It is one of several gnostic gospels that fell out of favor and were lost for nearly 1700 years.

Imperative Pleasures of Coastal Somalia. In November 2008, thirteen-year-old Aisha Ibrahim Duhulow (1995–2008) was stoned to death by fifty Al-Shabaab militants in a stadium in Kismayu, Somalia in front of a thousand spectators. Several bystanders tried to intervene but were shot at by the militants. She was accused of adultery in violation of "religious" law after she reported being raped. None of the men she accused of rape were arrested. Duhulow arrived to Kismayu with her family three months earlier from the Hagadera refugee camp in Kenya, which at the time was among the largest refugee camps in the world. According to Amnesty International, at one point during the stoning "nurses were instructed to check whether [Duhulow] was still alive . . . They removed her from the ground, declared that she was, and she was replaced in the hole where she had been buried for the stoning to continue."

Words in a Dead Girl's Mouth. Ten-year-old Kathina Thomas (1998–2008) was killed as she played in front of her home on May 29, 2008, in the West Hill neighborhood of Albany, New York. The single stray bullet that struck her in the back was indiscriminately fired by fifteen-year-old Jermayne Timmons (1993–) who was sentenced to fifteen years to life in prison, the maximum sentence allowed to a juvenile; in December 2022, he was granted an early parole. Firearms are the leading cause of death for children and adolescents in the United States.

The Wreck of the Unknown. A quadruplex, see note on "Terms of Surrender." With homage to *The Wreck of the Deutschland* by Gerard Manley Hopkins (1844–1889). Pauper graveyards in Mexico refer to the unidentified bodies of drowned migrants as *el desconocido* (the unknown). In 2019, according to the United Nations, there were 272 million international migrants, and 75.9 million people worldwide were forcibly displaced. The number of migrants outpaces the growth of the world's population.

For the Kingdom to Be Well. The siege of Leningrad by Nazi German forces began September 8, 1941 and lasted 872 days. It was the longest and most destructive siege in European history. The Soviet army suffered 3.5 million casualties, with over one million killed, captured, or missing. Nearly 200,000 civilians were killed mostly by starvation.

Mike Tyson Explains Middle Age to John Keats. John Keats (1795–1821) was prone to fighting as a youth, and his friends believed he was fated for a life in the military. Unlike most of his literary contemporaries, Keats had an impoverished childhood. At twenty years old, Mike Tyson (1966–) became the youngest person to ever win a heavyweight boxing title. To Nicole Tong (1979–).

Etymology of Hedberg's Escalator. Comedian Mitch Hedberg (1968–2005). Gene Kelly (1912–1996) had a fever during the filming of the title performance in the 1952 musical *Singing in the Rain*. The scene was shot over two and a half days, during which Kelly's fever peaked at 103. To Brian Nussbaum (1980–).

What Monsters You Make of Them. The title is from *Hamlet* (Act 3, Scene 1), where Hamlet insults Ophelia and accuses her of deceit. The first and third subtitles are taken from *De Rerum Natura* (The Nature of Things) by Lucretius (99 BC–55 BC).

The Quieting Muses. John Coltrane (1926–1967) replaced Sonny Rollins (1930–) in the Miles Davis (1926–1991) Quintet in 1955 and played with the band until 1960.

The Nine Mayan Gods of the Underworld Explain Delusions to John Roberts. There were nine gods of the underwold according to the nine books of *Chilam Balam*, the "books of the jaguar priest," from the 17th and 18th century that compile Mayan knowledge of history, religion, literature, astronomy, and medicine. These texts incorporate some traditions influenced by the 16th centrury Spanish conquests, and they are written in the Yucatec Maya language using a Latin alphabet. The heavy usage of Yucatec idioms and metaphors make translations exceedingly complex; and given that the majority of pre-Columbian Mayan texts were destroyed by Catholic missionaries, it is difficult to know what differentiates these gods. It is likely more than nine books originally existed.

Calculations on the Known World after the Garden of Eden. As told by C.B. Baugher II (1953–), barbecue maestro born and raised in Elkton, Virginia.

Like Shining from Shook Foil. The title is from *God's Grandeur* by Gerard Manley Hopkins (1844–1889). On December 12, 1911, the Morner family was murdered on their dairy farm in East Greebush, New York. Their bodies had been mutilated by a hatchet and buried in a manure pit and under the barn floorboards. The youngest child had been raped. The police launched a manhunt and offered a large reward for a farmhand who had been employed by the family. The farmhand was never found and the case went unsolved.

Etymology of the Ancient City. On March 29, 1516, the Venetian Republic imposed a forced segregation of the city's Jewish residents. By the early 17th century, this area of the city was know as "il ghetto," and established the term as a section of a city where a minority group is required to live. Il ghetto remained until 1797, when Napoleon Bonaparte conqueed the Venetian Republic and abolished the segregation laws.

We Call It Wisdom. The Battle of Towton was fought on March 29, 1461 (Palm Sunday) in Yorkshire, England. It was the culminating battle of the English War of the Roses between the royal houses of Lancaster and York. It is believed to be the longest, bloodiest, and largest battle ever fought on English soil.

Reading Nadezhda Mandelstam in Virgin Islands National Park. Virgin Islands National Park comprises nearly 60% of the 19.6 square miles of the island of Saint John. The island has no airport. Nadezhda Mandelstam's (1899–1980) memoirs of her life in the Soviet Union with her husband Osip Mandelstam (1891–1938) and after his murder are masterpieces of nonfiction. Osip Mandelstam's poems were banned throughout much of his adult life; many of his poems survived only because Nadezhda committed them to memory.

Emina R. Explains the Reflected Past to Christian Teresi. Emina R. (1988–) was my student at Albany High School in Albany, New York. According to art historian Rebecca Quinn Teresi (1988–), at a masked jousting tournament in honor of the Virgin in 1618, a student from Madrid offered prizes for the winners, among which were a plumed cap, a golden ring, and six yards of the finest silk. Much more interesting, however, was the prize doled out to the knight determined the loser: "Al que peor lo hiziere, un espejo en que se mire." Which is to say, if you were deemed the worst, you were awarded a mirror to look at yourself.

Metamorphoses. The Naga are an ethnic group of numerous tribes that reside in northeastern India and northwestern Myanmar. They speak more than twenty distinct Tibeto-Burman languages and share similar cultures and traditions. Headhunting was a ritual meant to symbolize courage and steal the power of enemies; it was a recorded practice among the Naga until 1969. Nagaland in India was an independent state before British colonial rule.

Reading Carlos Drummond de Andrade in Everglades National Park. It is theorized the alligator that killed two-year-old Nebraskan, Lane Graves, at Walt Disney World on June 14, 2016, may have been handfed and lost its fear of humans because it lived near a densely populated area. Having no way to easily identify the alligator that killed the boy, the Florida Fish and Wildlife Commission was forced to capture and euthanize six from the area.

Encomium Post Requiem. To Jaimie Holmes (1985–).

Sibylline. To Sibyl Philo (1945–2020), who knew nature was her religion.

To Burn the Autocrat in Effigy. To Anastasia Strokina (1984–). The phrase "thin-necked deputies" is from Osip Mandelstam's poem "The Stalin Epigram."

Ruth Stone Explains the Book of the Dead to Sylvia Plath. Ruth Stone (1915–2011) was one of my undergraduate professors at Binghamton University. When living in England with her husband, the writer Walter Stone (1917–1959), they were invited to dinner with Sylvia Plath (1932–1963) and Ted Hughes (1930–1998), but had to cancel when Ruth got sick. Shortly after, Walter committed suicide by hanging. Ruth never met Plath or Hughes.

ACKNOWLEDGMENTS

I am grateful to the editors of the following publications where these poems, often in different forms, appeared. *AGNI*: "The Wreck of the Unknown"; *American Poetry Review*: "Encomium Post Requiem"; *Blackbird*: "Words in a Dead Girl's Mouth"; *The Café Review*: "Metamorphosis"; *Copper Nickel*: "Imperative Pleasures of Coastal Somalia"; *Crab Orchard Review*: "For the Kingdom to Be Well"; *DIAGRAM*: "Climb a Tree, Take a Swim, Kiss a Woman," "Emina R. Explains the Reflected Past to Christian Teresi," and "Etymology of Hedberg's Escalator"; *The Literary Review*: "Sonny Rollins Explains the Apocrypha to Judas"; *Misrepresented People: Poetic Responses to Trump's America* (New York Quarterly Books): "Etymology of the Ancient City," "The Nine Mayan Gods of the Underworld Explain Delusions to John Roberts"; *Narrative*: "Mike Tyson Explains Middle Age to John Keats," "The Nine Mayan Gods of the Underworld Explain Delusions to John Roberts," "Ruth Stone Explains the Book of the Dead to Sylvia Plath"; *Nimrod International Journal*: "What Monsters You Make of Them"; *On the Seawall*: "Reading Nadezhda Mandelstam in Virgin Islands National Park"; *Pine Hills Review*: "Reading Osip Mandelstam in Zion National Park"; *Revolver*: "Like Shining from Shook Foil"; *Shrew*: "We Call It Wisdom"; *South Dakota Review*: "Reading Carlos Drummond de Andrade in Everglades National Park"; *Swamp Pink*: "To Burn the Autocrat in Effigy"; and *TriQuarterly*: "An Alternate Version of Goya's *The Dog*."

I have been fortunate to study with exceptional mentors, and this book owes an enduring debt to Jennifer Atkinson, Paul-William Burch, David Fenza, Carolyn Forché, Eric Pankey, Liz Rosenberg, and Ruth Stone for their time and faith.

Thank you to the colleagues and friends, too many to name, whose support and advice was essential over the many years it took to write these poems, but especially Lana Austin, Josh Baugher, Sheila Black, Brian Brodeur, Matt Burriesci, Katie Claire, Kiley Cogis Brodeur, J.K. Daniels, Danielle Cadena Deulen, Dante Di Stefano, Jay Duda, Shanley Jacobs, Erin Kemper Burriesci, Denise Low, J. Michael Martinez, Christopher Merrill, Melanie McCabe, Nancy Pearson, Chris Perkowski, Dave Rothman, Steve Scafidi, Kevin Stoy, Tree Swenson, Nicole Tong, Emily Tuszynska, and Margaret Yocom. A particular thanks to my fellow participants of the Heritage Workshop at George Mason University. Thank you to the Washington, DC Commission on the Arts and Humanities for their generosity.

My deepest appreciation to Mark Cull, Kate Gale, Tobi Harper Petrie, and everyone at Red Hen Press for tirelessly advocating for literature and creating space for this book to exist. And to my family, nice and easy, Gregory Teresi, Margaret Kennedy, Nina Teresi, Jerry Teresi, and Joseph Teresi, who always encouraged me in this strange and wonderous pursuit. Я тебя люблю, Jaimie Holmes, the truest compass I know.

AUTHOR BIO

Christian Teresi is a poet, essayist, and translator whose work has been published in many journals, including *AGNI,* the *American Poetry Review, Blackbird*, the *Kenyon Review*, the *Literary Review, Literary Hub, Narrative*, and *Subtropics*. His work has been supported by a fellowship from the DC Commission on the Arts and Humanities. He holds degrees from Binghamton University and George Mason University. Born in Albany, New York, he currently lives in Washington, DC, where he works on international education and public diplomacy initiatives.

Printed in the USA
CPSIA information can be obtained
at www.ICGtesting.com
JSHW060142120724
66318JS00003B/3